MW01049721

KEENELAND *Now*

CREATED AND PRODUCED BY
FRAN TAYLOR & MATT ANDERSON

KEENELAND®
Keeneland Association, Inc.
Lexington, KY 40588-1690
www.keeneland.com

EP
ECLIPSE
PRESS
Lexington, KY 40513
www.eclipsepress.com

Copyright © 2010 Keeneland Association, Inc.
LEXINGTON, KY 40588-1690
WWW.KEENELAND.COM

All rights reserved. No part of this book may be reproduced in
any form by any means, including photocopying, audio recording,
or any information storage or retrieval system, without the
permission in writing from the copyright holder. Inquiries should
be addressed to Publisher, Blood-Horse Publications, Box 919003,
Lexington, KY 40591-9003.

Library of Congress Control Number: 2009941422

ISBN 978-1-58150-335-7
Printed in China
Design by Fran Taylor & Matt Anderson

A KEENELAND LEGACY PRODUCT

*All profits from the sale of this item will be contributed to qualified non-profit organizations
through the Keeneland Foundation. By making a purchase, you will also be making an
investment in the future of central Kentucky. We are pleased to give you this opportunity
to share in the heritage of Keeneland.*

Acknowledgments

No doubt about it, Keeneland is a special place. Despite its scenic beauty and obvious charms, it is very difficult for any photographer to capture the magic of Keeneland. It requires the right light, moment in time, weather, and, of course, subject matter. Furthermore, it is not just one shot or several. It takes many wonderful shots and lots of talented photographers to convey adequately that which is special about Keeneland.

Over the years there have been countless amateur and professional photographers chronicling the history and traditions of Keeneland. Shooting great vistas and the smallest details, they have been in the perfect spot, had the sense, talent, and sometimes good luck to click the shutter and capture the moment. This book showcases Keeneland's own collection of photographs.

Special thanks goes to Keeneland staff photographer Matt Anderson for his twin skills as photographer/graphic designer and his dedication to this project. A team headed by Enzina Mastrippolito (Photos by Z) provided a number of great shots documenting *KEENELAND Now*. A beautiful sunrise at the starting gate by G. D. Hieronymus, Keeneland's director of broadcast services, is proof that his stills are as powerful as his videos.

The magnificent photo collection in the Keeneland Library made *KEENELAND Then* possible. Brownie Leach, Skeets Meadors, and John Wyatt were some of the photographers who preserved the past so we could enjoy it forever. We were happy to include one very special moment captured by legendary equine photographer Tony Leonard.

Cathy Schenck and Phyllis Rogers have safeguarded the Keeneland Library collections that Amelia Buckley first organized. Very special thanks goes to Amy Petit, who bridged the gap between the Keeneland Library photo collections and the digital divide, creating a database that made the search for the best photos of the past far more manageable for this and future projects.

— Fran Taylor, Executive Director
Keeneland Foundation

APPROACHING FIRST TURN / M. Anderson

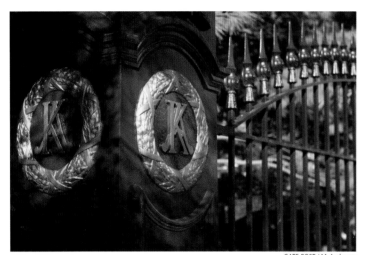

GATE POST / M. Anderson

FLAG / M. Anderson

TIME TO RACE / Photos by Z

SILKS ROOM / M. Anderson

BREAKING / Photos by Z

AND THEY'RE OFF / Photos by Z

LORDY WINS / Photos by Z

WINNERS / Photos by Z

MEETING A REAL JOCKEY / M. Anderson

WINNING COLORS / M. Anderson

SYCAMORE / Photos by Z

FIRST TURN / Photos by Z

PARASOL / Photos by Z

OUTRIDER WAITS / M. Anderson

TAKING FLIGHT / PHOTOS BY Z

MORNING WORK / M. Anderson

JOCKEYING FOR POSITION / Photos by Z

JUNIOR JOCKEY / M. Anderson

PADDOCK PLAY / Photos by Z

PINK MUMS / M. Anderson

GIRL IN PINK / Photos by Z

YELLOW RIDER / Photos by Z

GOLDEN MUMS / Photos by Z

PACKED APRON / Photos by Z

JOCKEYS TALK / M. Anderson

MAKING PICKS / Photos by Z

BLUE BUTTERFLY / M. Anderson

LITTLE DUDE / Photos by Z

GREEN HAT / Photos by Z

BIG PINK HAT / Photos by Z

PINK HAT / Photos by Z

BLACK HAT / Photos by Z

POST PARADE / Photos by Z

BUCKY SALLEE / M. Anderson

HARROWING THE TRACK / M. Anderson

SPECTATOR / Photos by Z

BUCKY BOOTS / M. Anderson

JOCKEY BOOTS / Photos by Z

WRAPS ON FENCE / Photos by Z

DARK GREY CLOSE UP / Photos by Z

RED SADDLETOWEL / Photos by Z

DAPPLED GREY / Photos by Z

TWO ICONS / M. Anderson

TRACTOR IN SNOW / M. Anderson

FALL COLOR / M. Anderson

REFLECTED FALL GLORY / M. Anderson

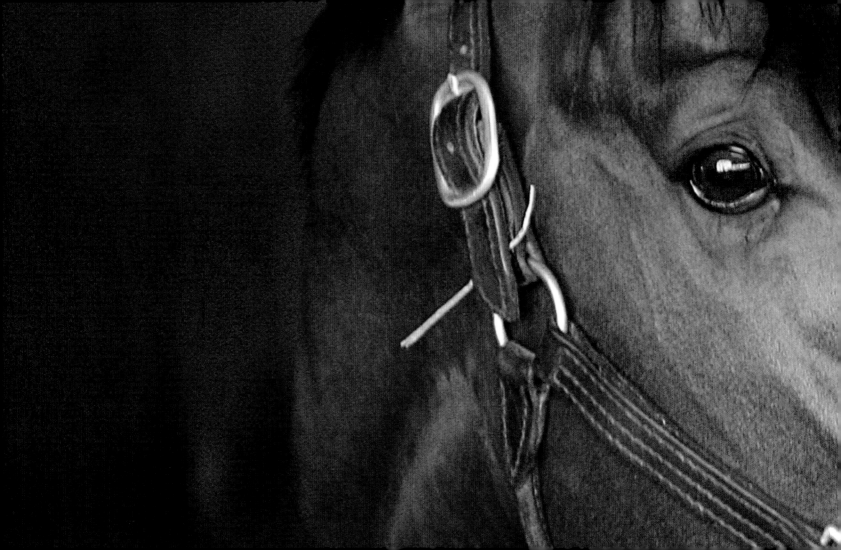

BROWN-EYED BEAUTY / Photos by Z

HIP NUMBER / M. Anderson

JANUARY SALE / M. Anderson

READY TO SELL / M. Anderson

KEENELAND SALES PAVILION / M. Anderson

SUNLIGHT INSPECTION / Photos by Z

BLUE BLANKET / Photos by Z

APRIL SALES PREVIEW / M. Anderson

SEPTEMBER SALES INSPECTION / M. Anderson

SCHOOLING AT THE GATE / G.D. Hieronymus

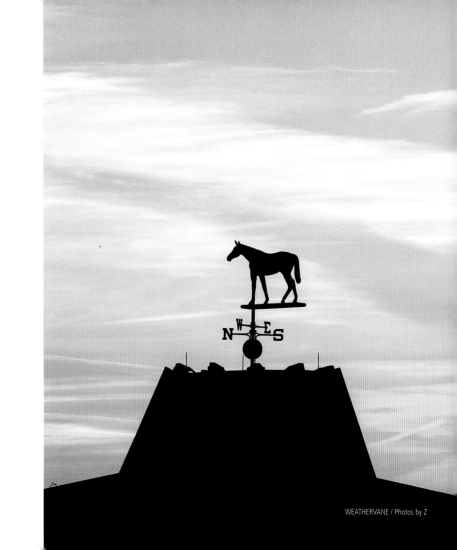

WEATHERVANE / Photos by Z

1970'S SALES ARENA / Keeneland Library

1968 YEARLING SALE / Keeneland Library

1950 SALES PAVILION / Keeneland Library

1950 AUCTIONEERS / Keeneland Library

1950 SALE / Keeneland Library

EARLY 60'S SALES / Keeneland Library

1943 SALE / Keeneland - Meadors

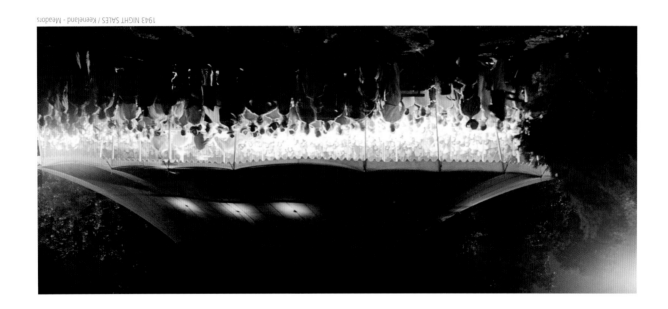

1943 SALES / Keeneland - Meadors

1943 FIRST SALE / Keeneland · Meadors

1978 ALYDAR / Keeneland – Leonard

1978 KEENELAND HEDGES / Keeneland Library

EARLY TRACK KITCHEN / Keeneland Library

1962 ANGUS / Keeneland - Meadors

1970 DOG SHOW / Keeneland - Wyatt

1962 CAR SHOW / Keeneland - Meadors

1962 ANGUS SHOW / Keeneland - Meadors

1960'S PONY CLUB / Keeneland - Wyatt

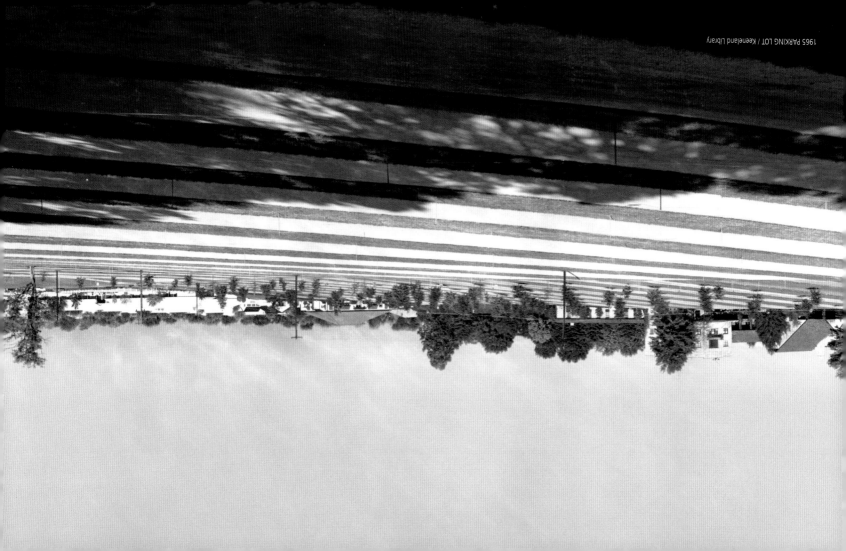

1965 PARKING LOT / Keeneland Library

1968 BUCKY SALLEE / Keeneland Library

1953 CLUB VIEW / Keeneland – Meadors

1966 PADDOCK / Keeneland - Meadors

1962 GATEPOST / Keeneland - Meadors

1941 CLUB LOBBY / Keeneland Library

1948 KEENELAND CROWD / Keeneland - Meadors

1957 H.P. HEADLEY, DUVAL HEADLEY, L.L. HAGGIN II / Keeneland Library

1938 KEENELAND HEDGE / Keeneland - Meadors

1942 OUTRIDER / Keeneland Library

1938 LEAVING THE TRACK / Keeneland Library

1936 COMBS & HEADLEY / Keeneland Library

1938 CLUB CROWD / Keeneland Library

1938 RAIL SITTERS / Keeneland Library

1949 CROWD / Keeneland - Meadors

1942 ASHLAND STAKES / Keeneland Library

C. 1935 - 1940 JOCKEYS / Keeneland Library

C. 1935 - 1940 JOCKEY STATUE / Keeneland Library

1940 POST PARADE / Keeneland - Leach

1936 OPENING DAY / Keeneland Library

1950 PADDOCK VIEW / Keeneland - Meadors

1938 - 1941 FINAL STRETCH / Keeneland Library

1946 RACING JUDGES / Keeneland Library

1936 PANORAMIC / Keeneland Library

1935 STONEWORK GRANDSTAND / Keeneland Library

1935 FRAMING / Keeneland Library

1935 BREAKING GROUND / Keeneland Library

I take this means of expressing my sincere appreciation to President Hal Price Headley and his associates in Keeneland Association for their perpetuating the name Keeneland in the organization of their Association and the race course they have built. It is a distinct honor to have the name of my family carried on in this manner.

In planning and starting a race course at Keeneland Stud it was my earnest hope to give to the Blue Grass and Kentucky, my native state, a place where sportsmen and sportswomen might some day gather and enjoy Thoroughbred racing in its finest form. Changing conditions make it impossible to fulfill that desire.

Keeneland Association, I am sure, will carry out those ideals of perpetuating Thoroughbred racing as a means of improving the Thoroughbred and of establishing a place where racing is conducted for sport.

To Keeneland Association I offer my sincerest congratulations and fervent hope for a successful future.

—— *John Oliver "Jack" Keene*
1936 Keeneland Race Meet Program

Copyright © 2010 Keeneland Association, Inc.
LEXINGTON, KY 40588-1690
WWW.KEENELAND.COM

All rights reserved. No part of this book may be reproduced in
any form by any means, including photocopying, audio recording,
or any information storage or retrieval system, without the
permission in writing from the copyright holder. Inquiries should
be addressed to Publisher, Blood-Horse Publications, Box 919003,
Lexington, KY 40591-9003.

Library of Congress Control Number: 2009941422

ISBN 978-1-58150-335-7
Printed in China
Design by Fran Taylor & Matt Anderson

A KEENELAND LEGACY PRODUCT

*All profits from the sale of this item will be contributed to qualified non-profit organizations
through the Keeneland Foundation. By making a purchase, you will also be making an
investment in the future of central Kentucky. We are pleased to give you this opportunity
to share in the heritage of Keeneland.*

KEENELAND *Then*

CREATED AND PRODUCED BY
FRAN TAYLOR & MATT ANDERSON

Keeneland Association, Inc.
Lexington, KY 40588-1690
www.keeneland.com

ECLIPSE
PRESS

Lexington, KY 40513
www.eclipsepress.com